Aggie Brazil's Christmas Colouring Book

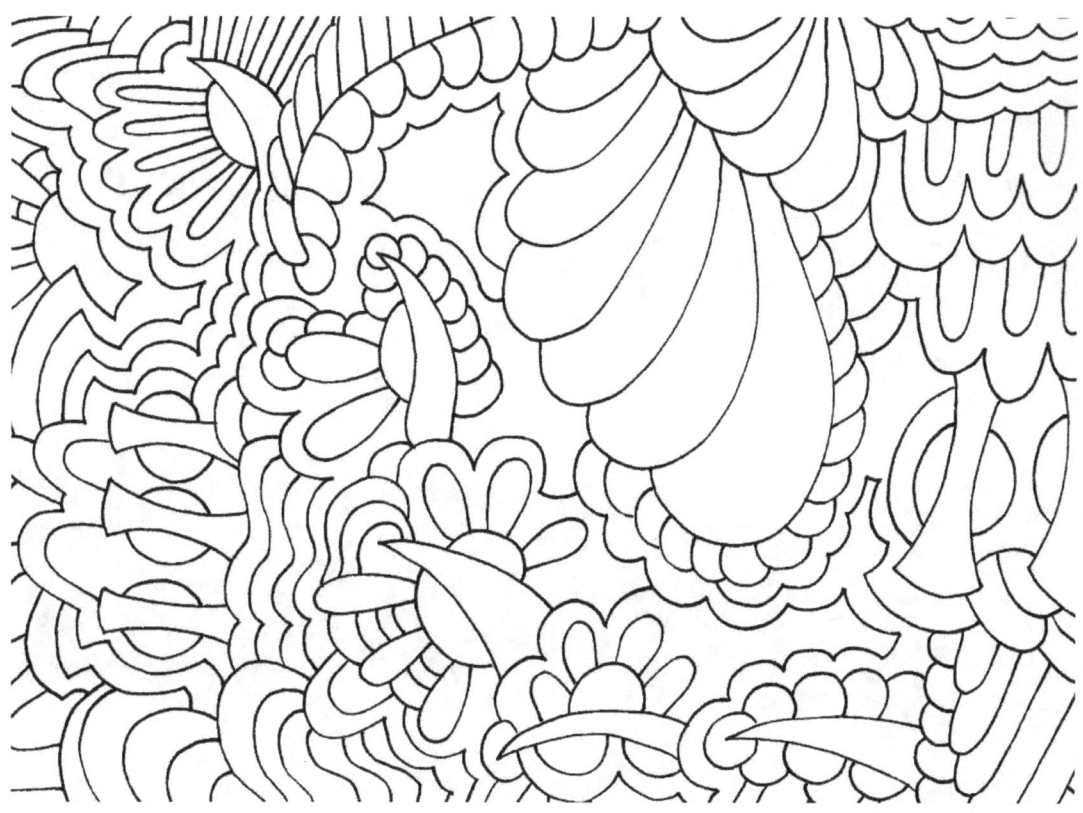

Copyright © 2016 Karen Woodhouse (Alias Aggie Brazil).
The rights of Karen Woodhouse (Aggie Brazil) to be identified as the illustrator of this work has been asserted by her in accordance with the Copyright, Designs and Patents Act 1988. All rights reserved, including the right of reproduction in whole or in any part, in any form.

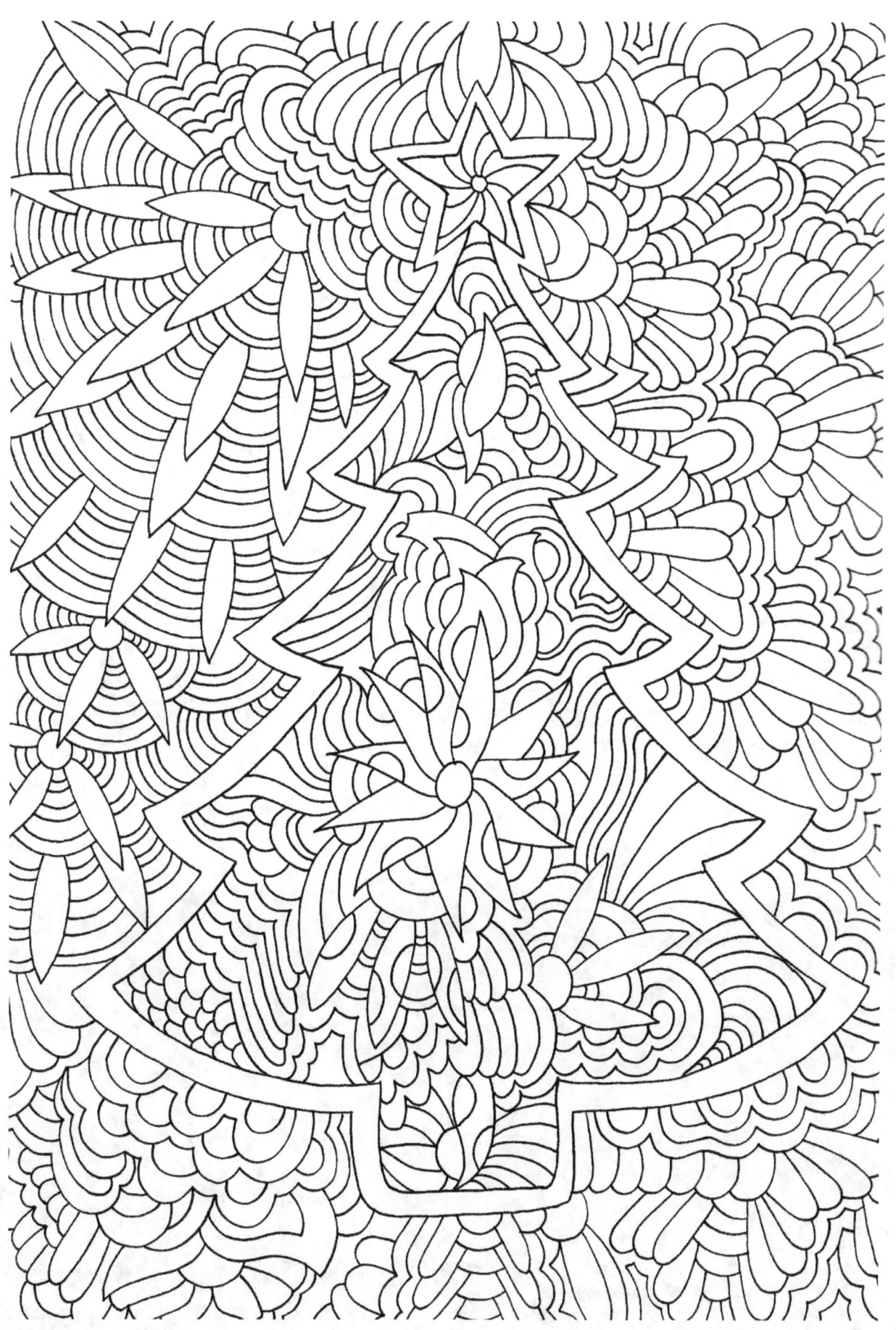

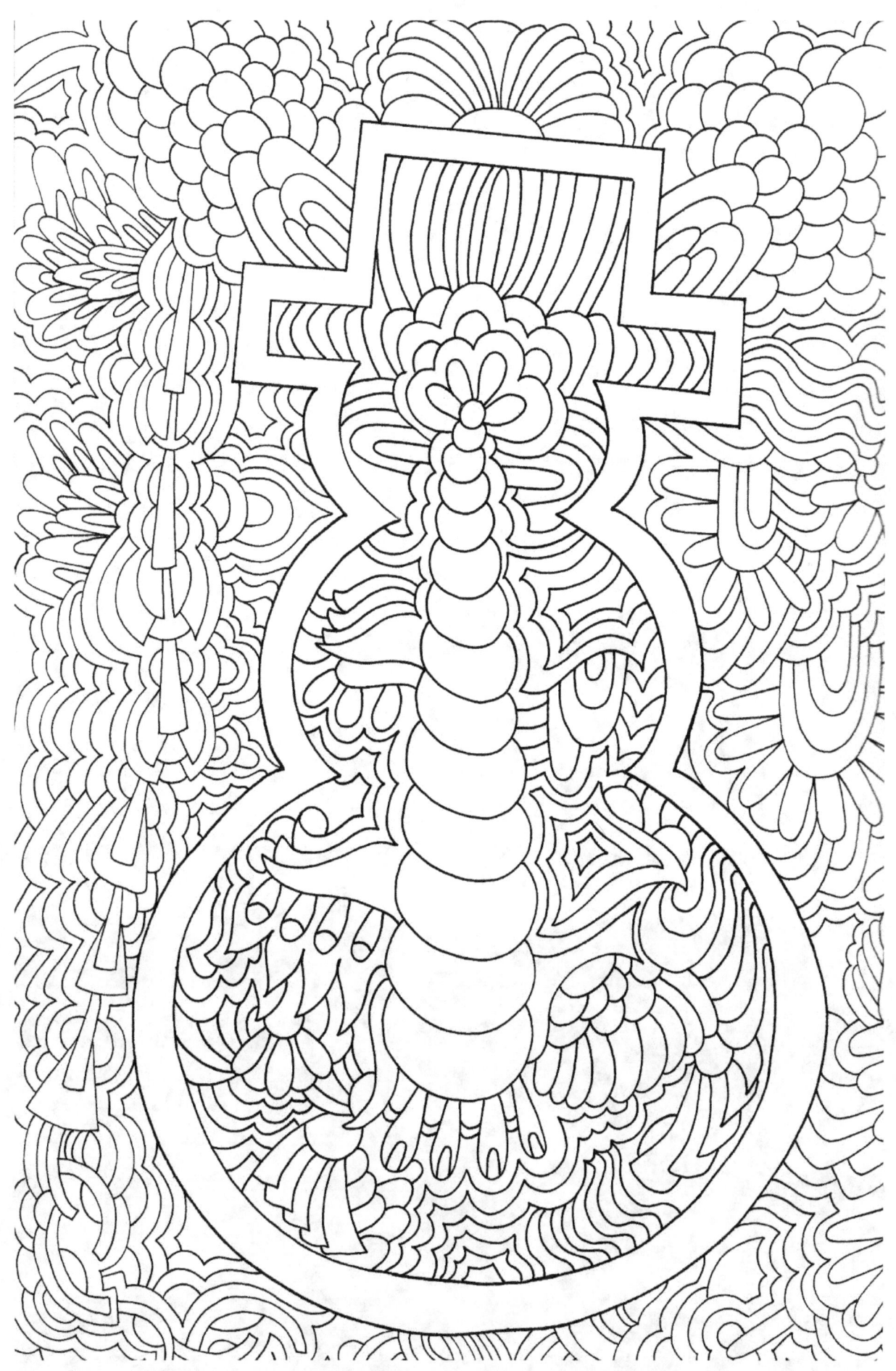

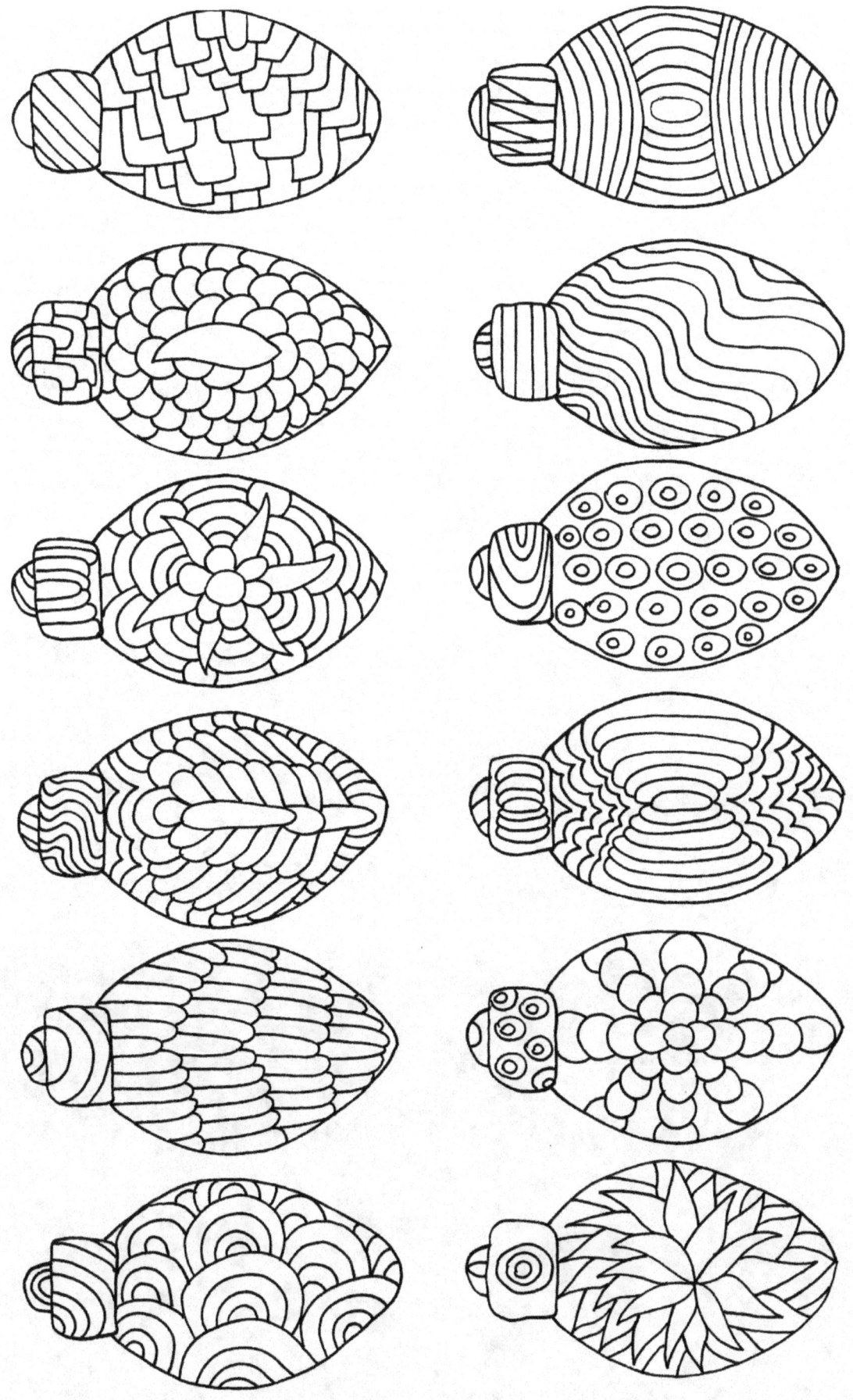

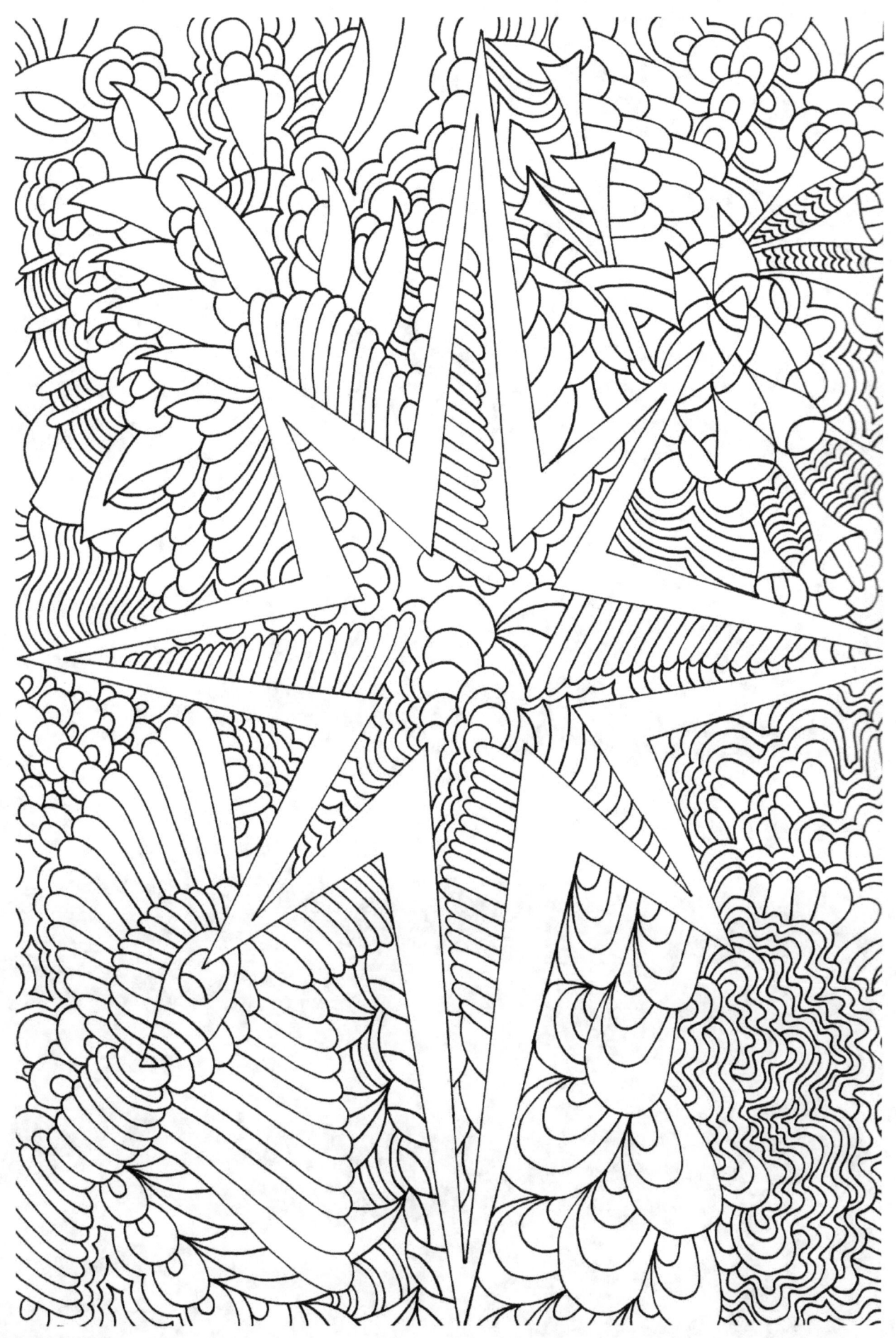

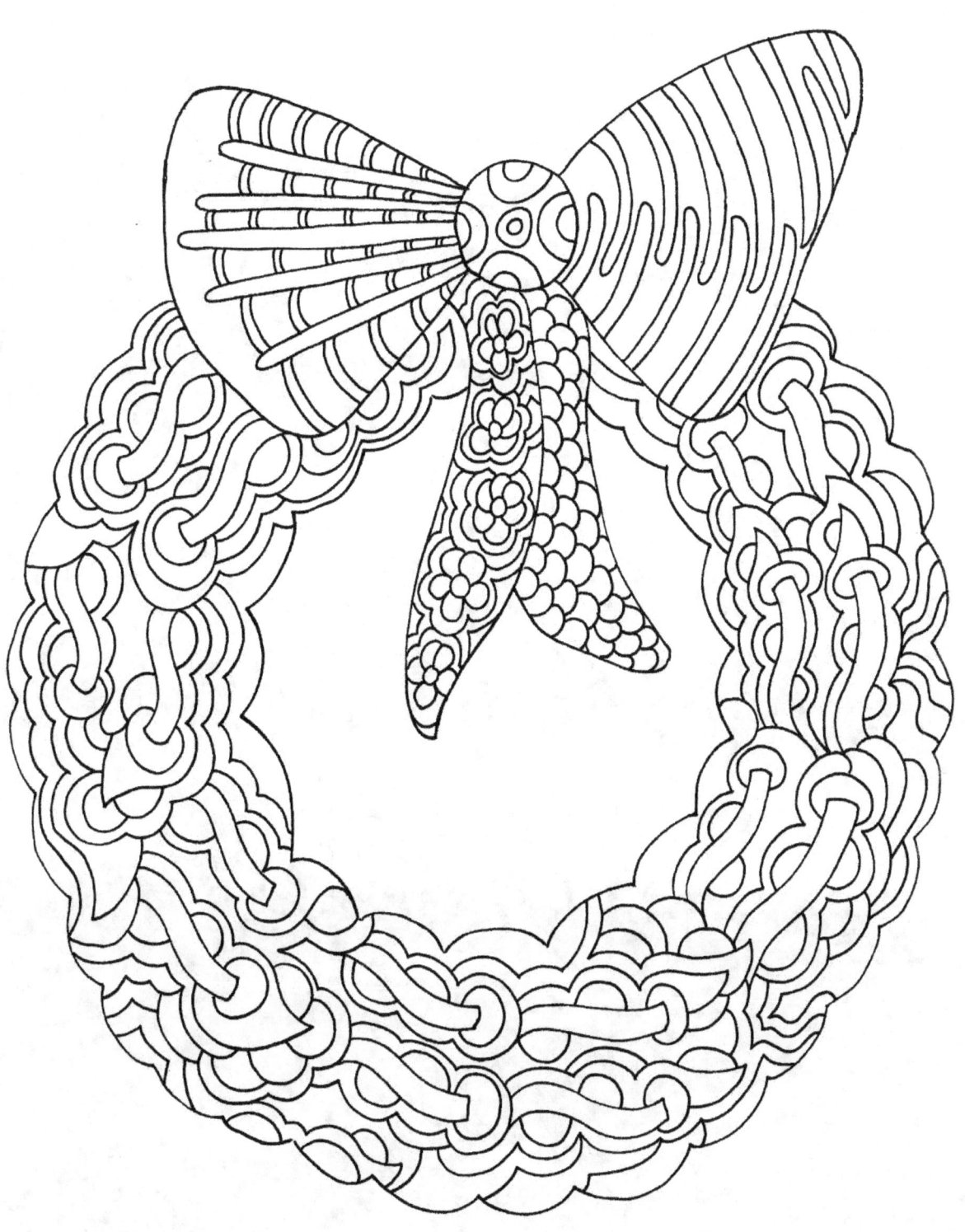

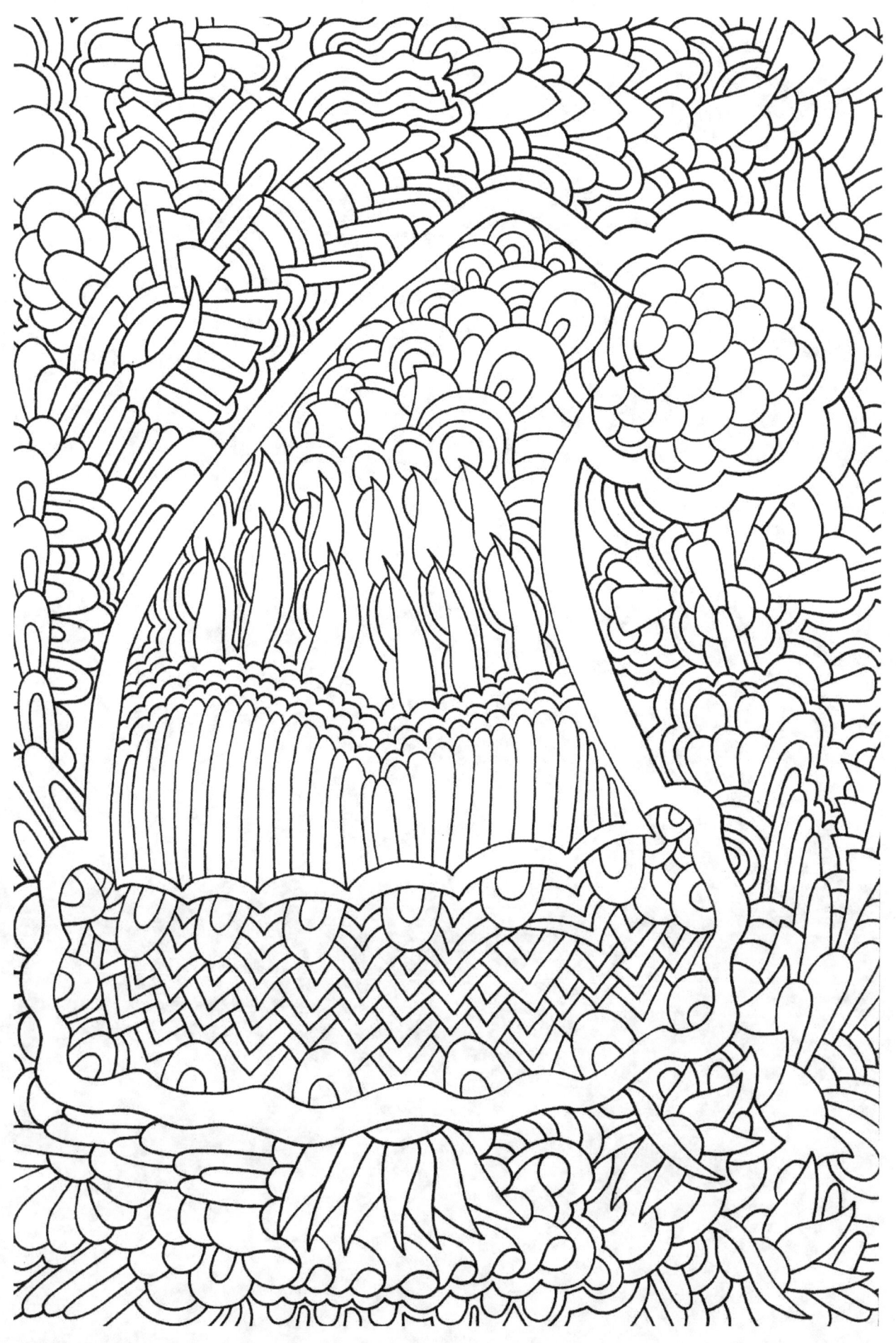

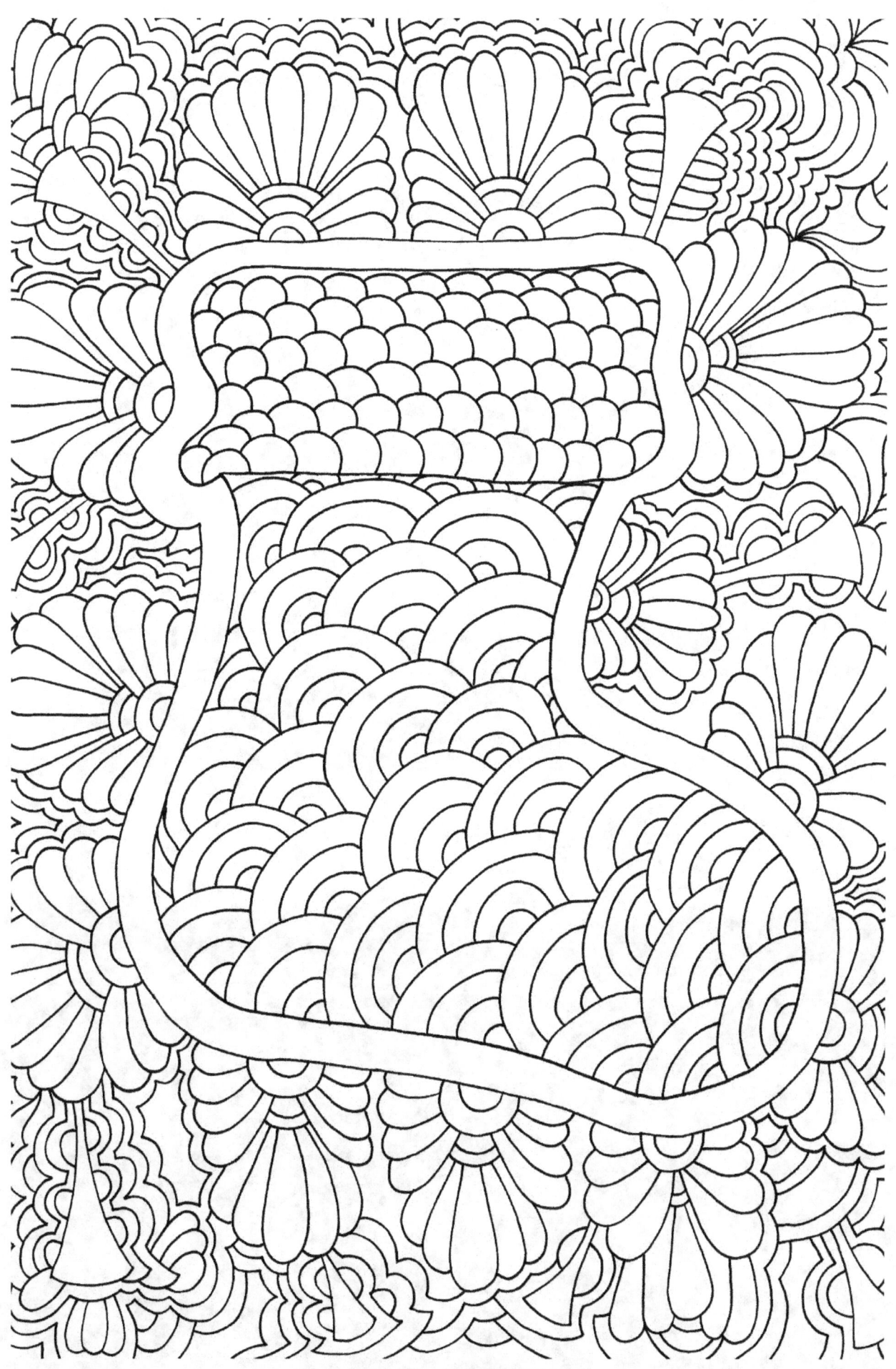

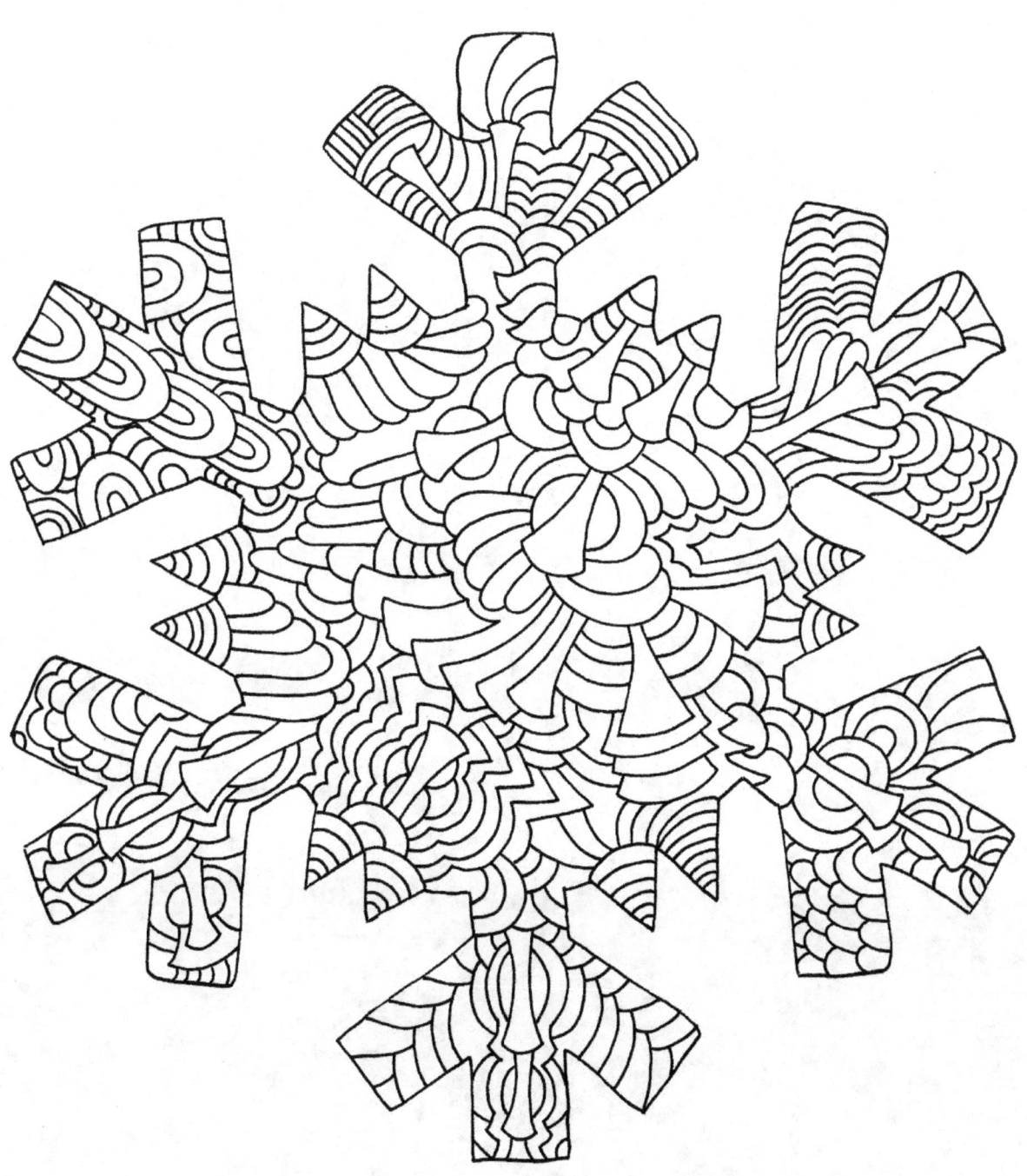

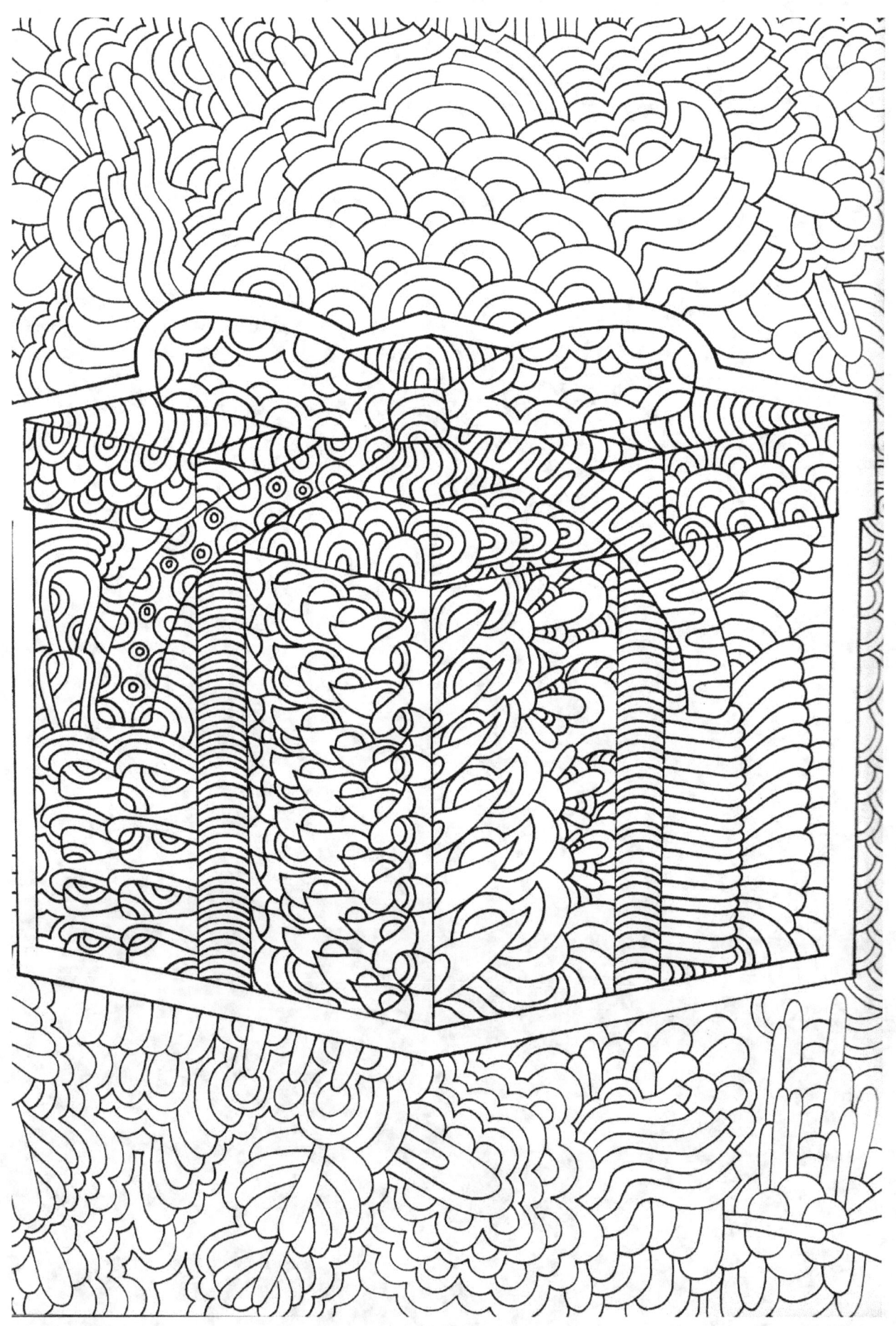

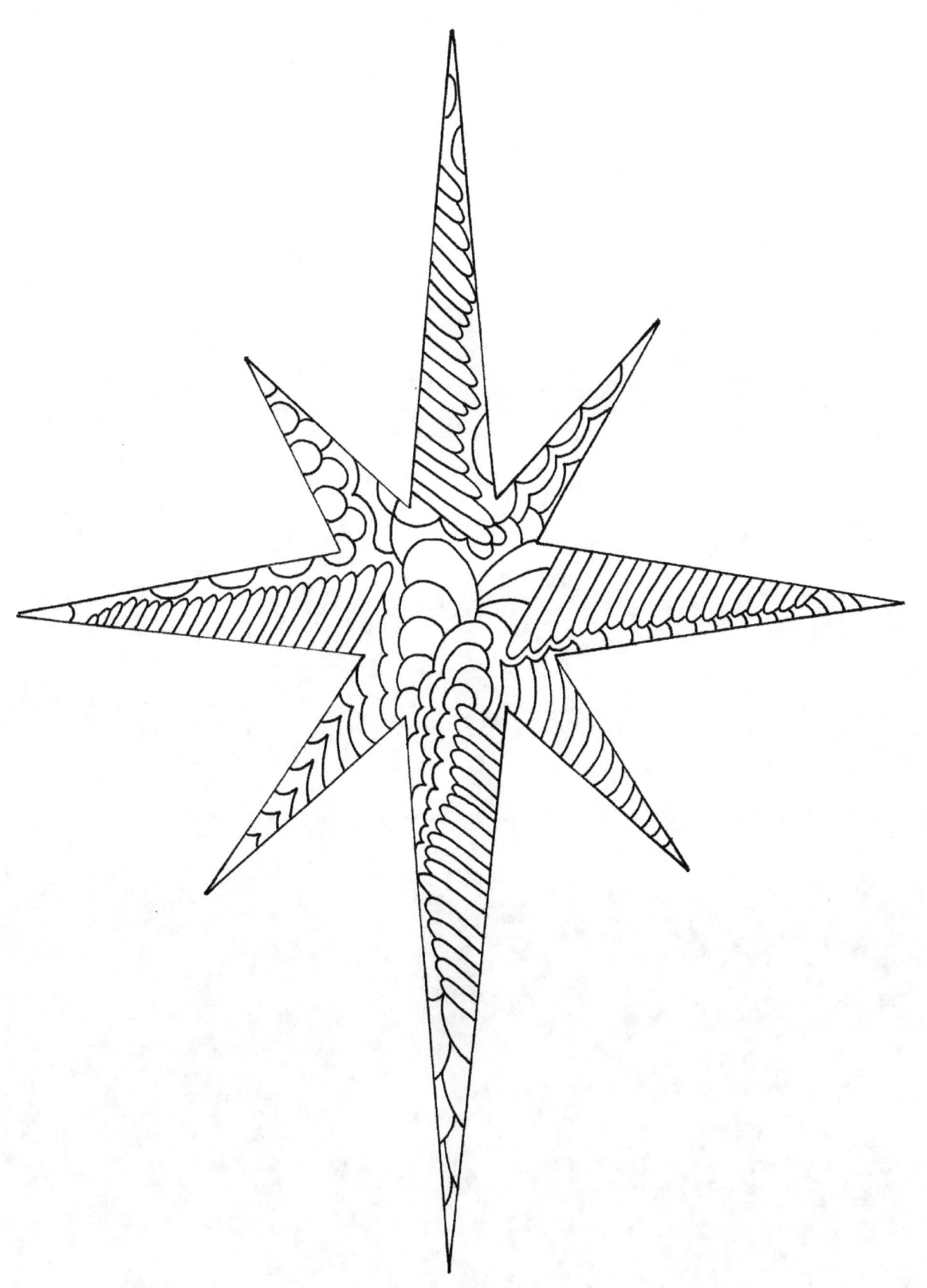

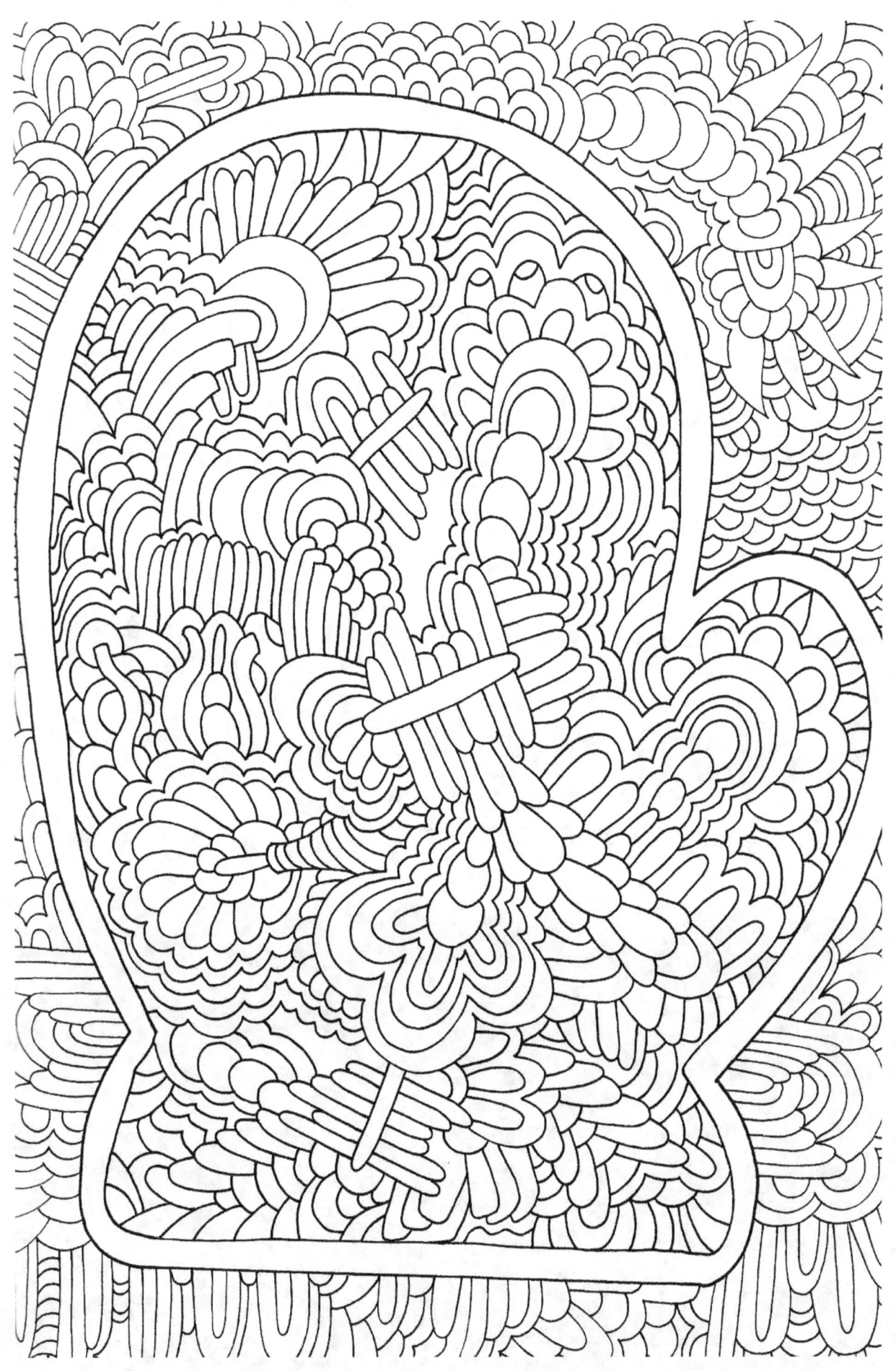

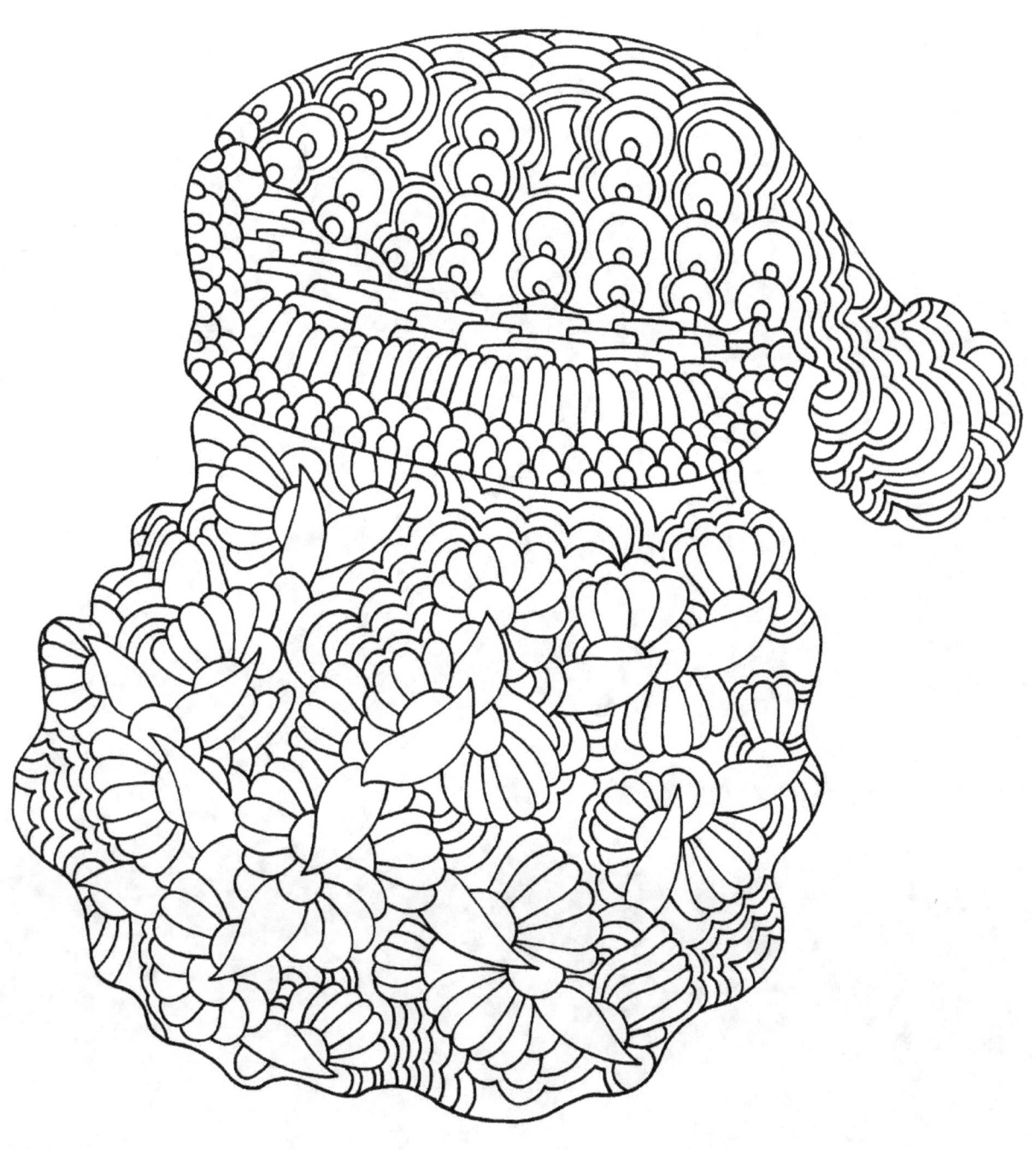

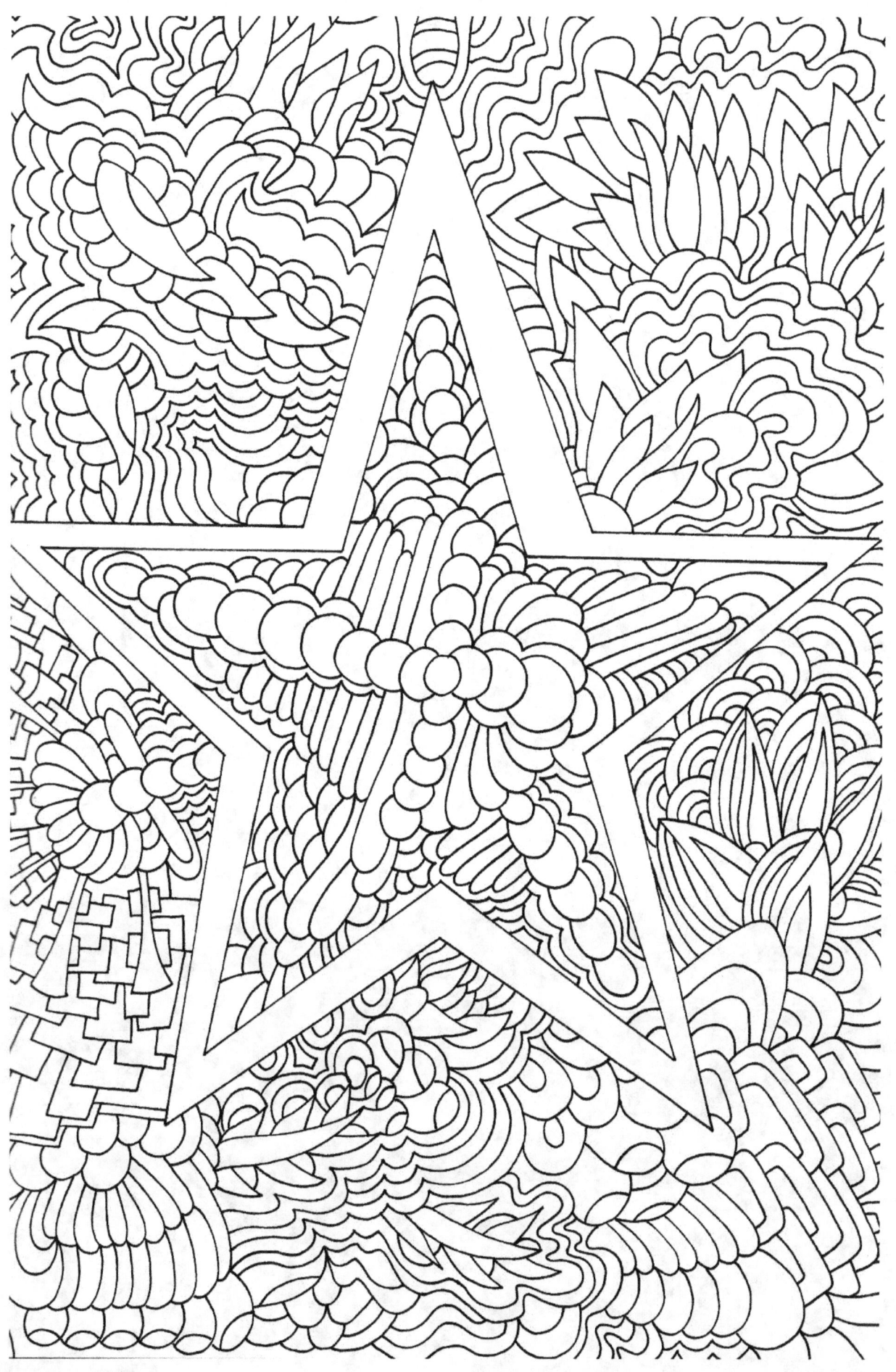

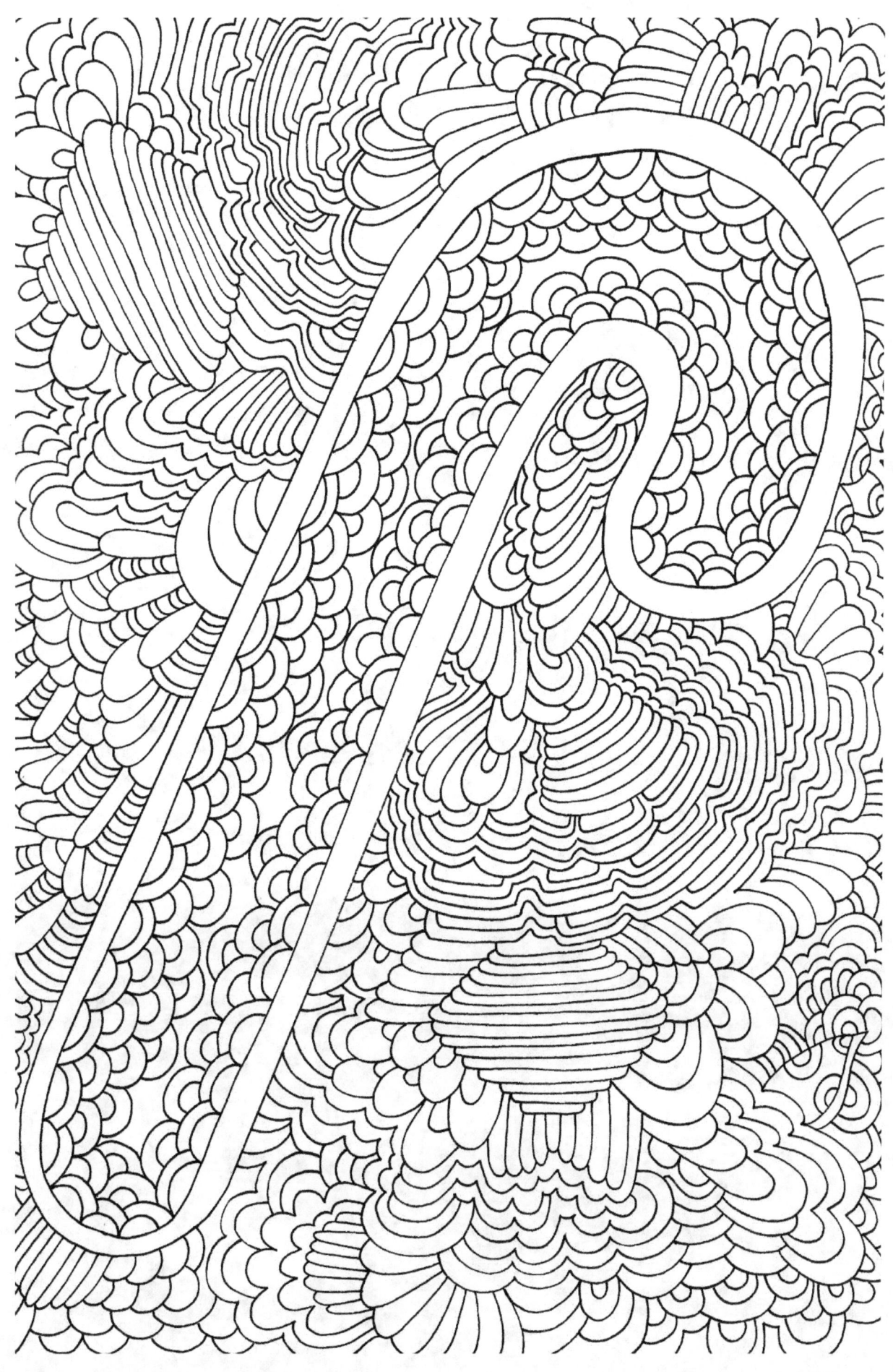

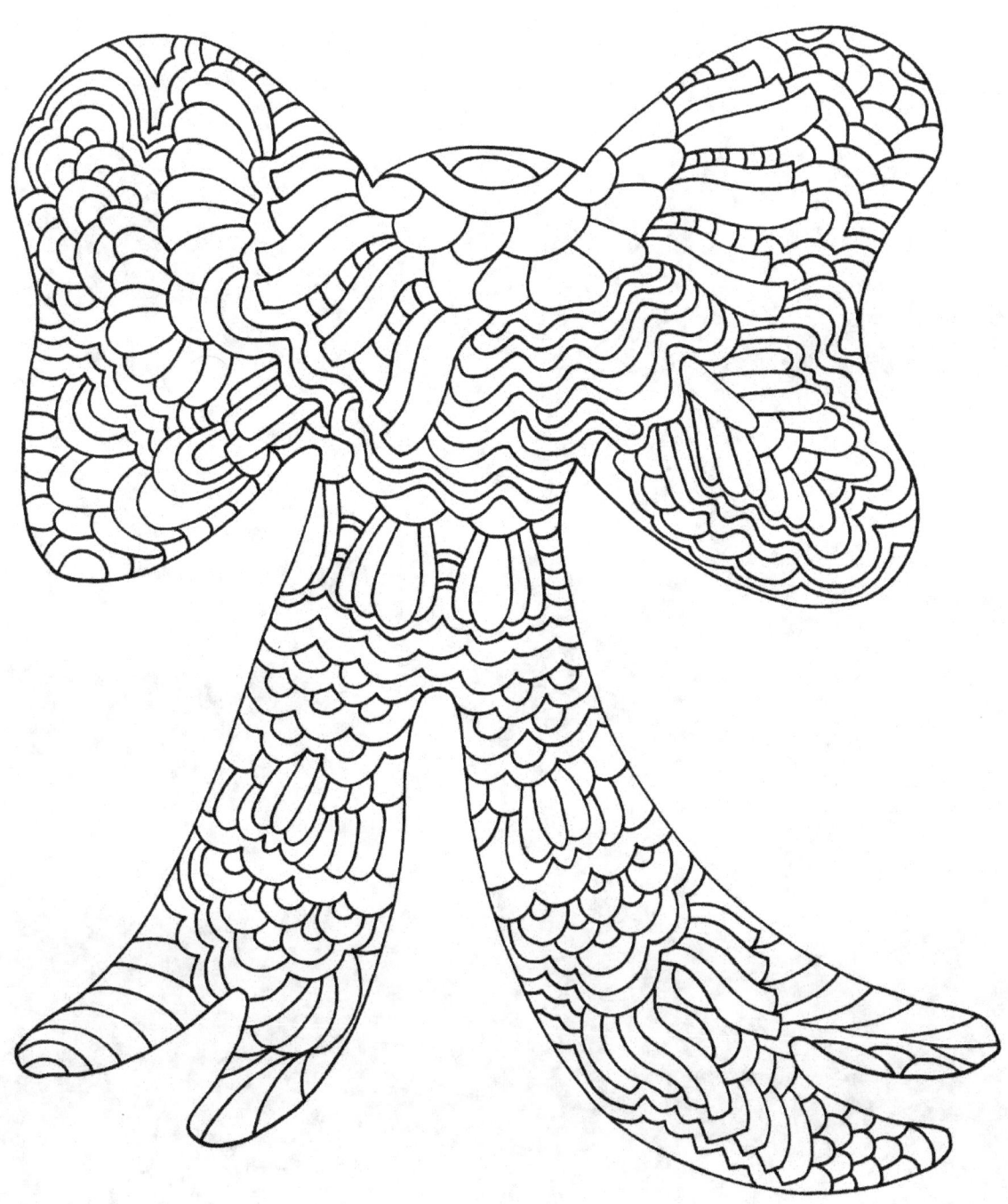

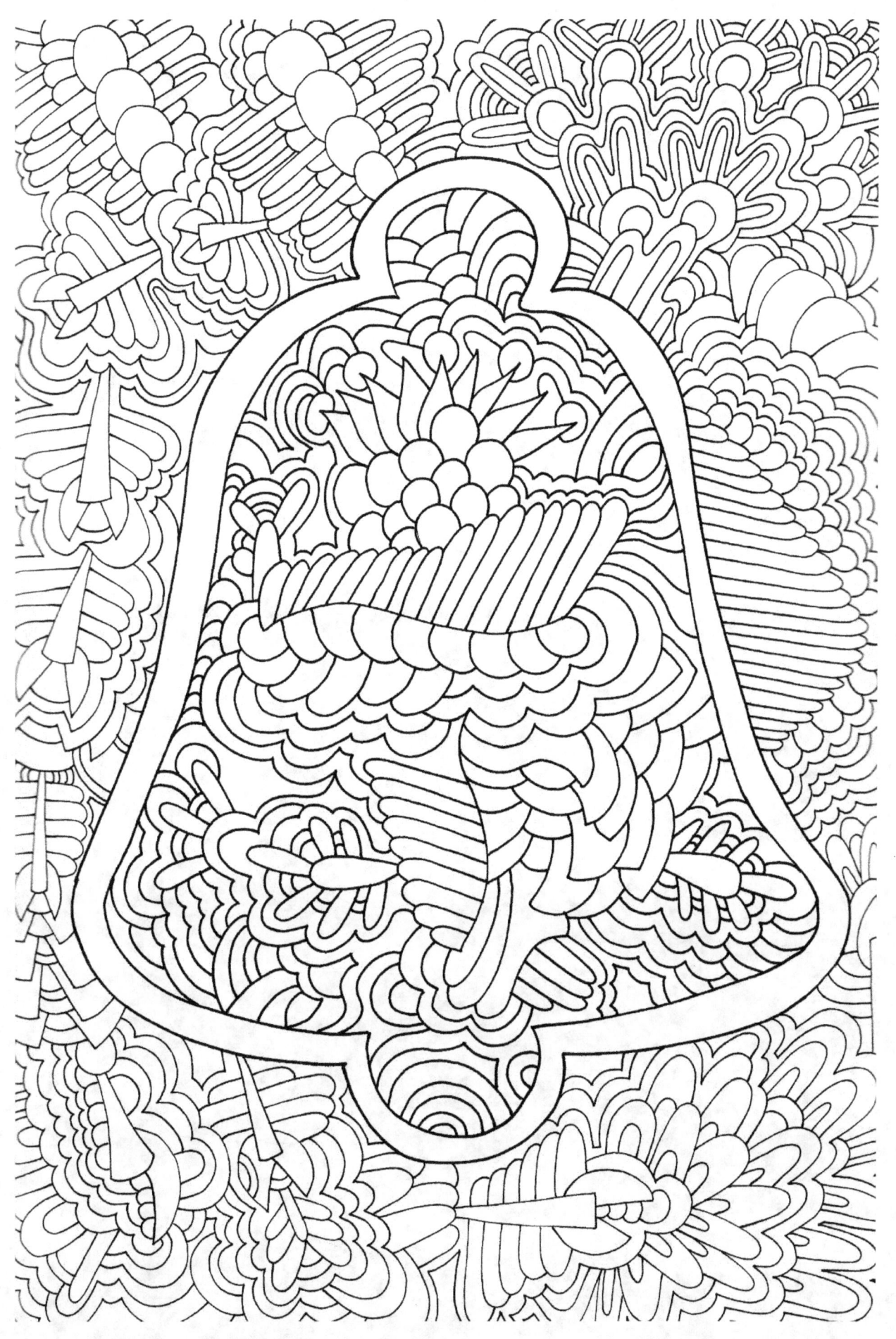

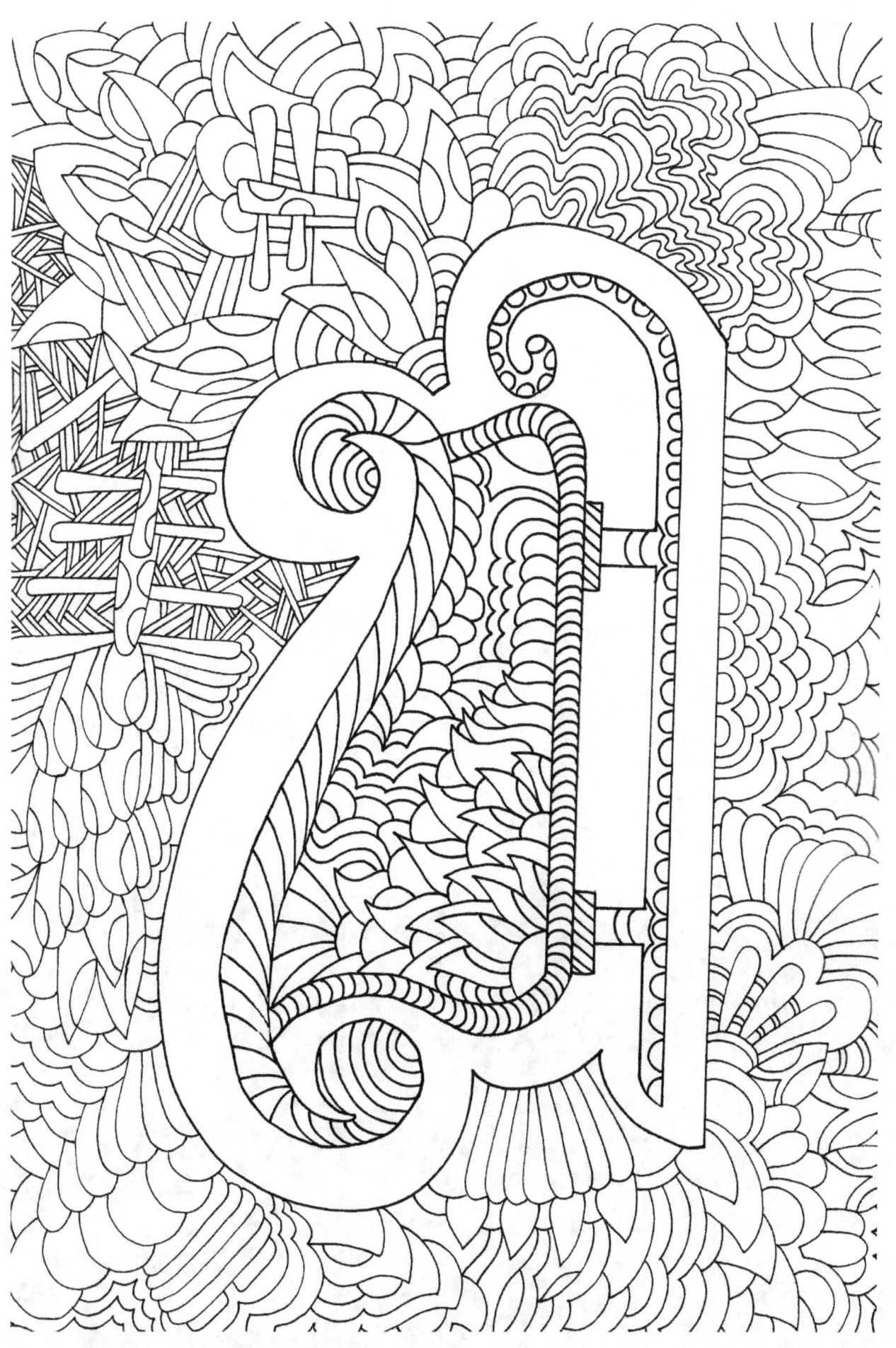

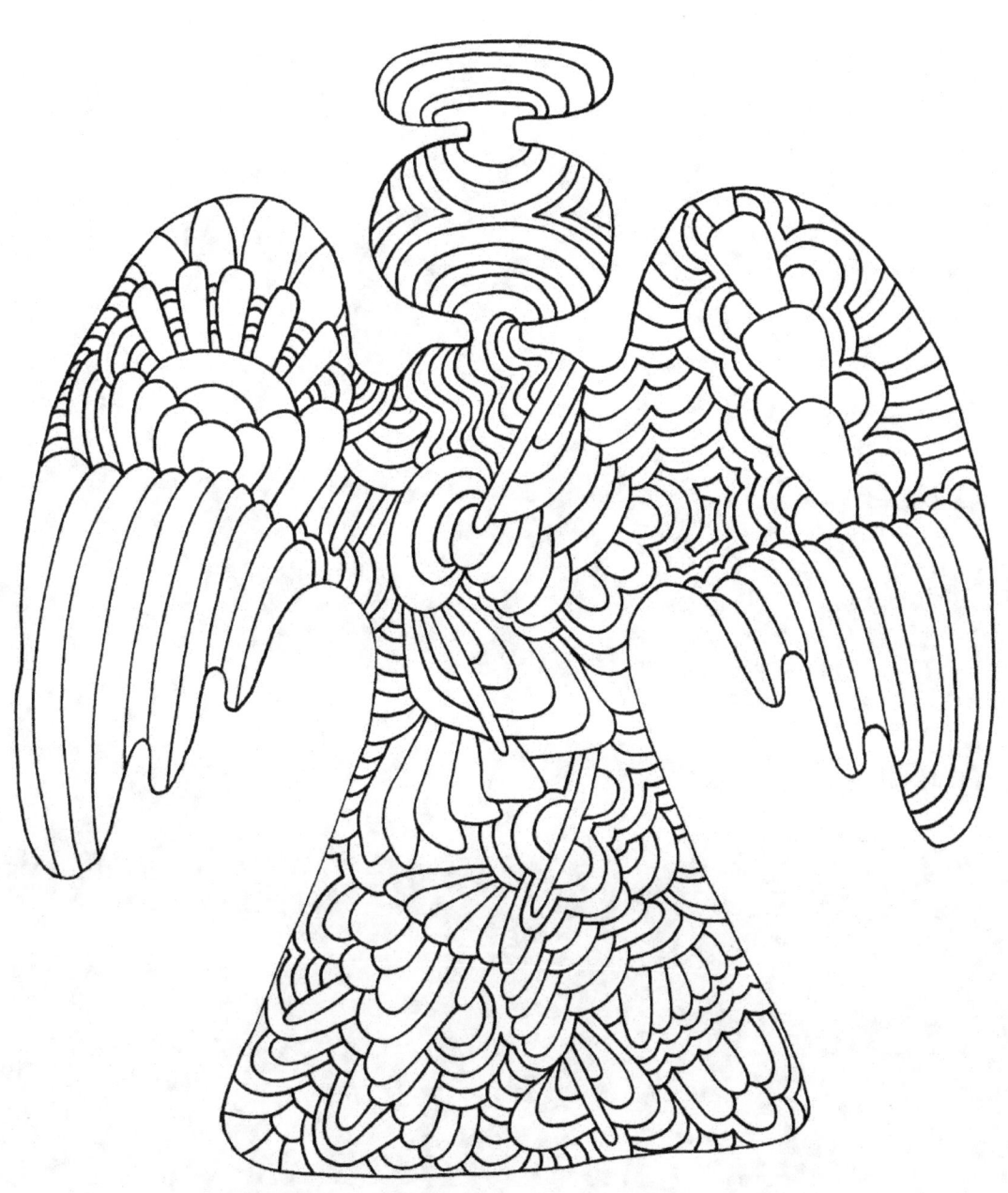

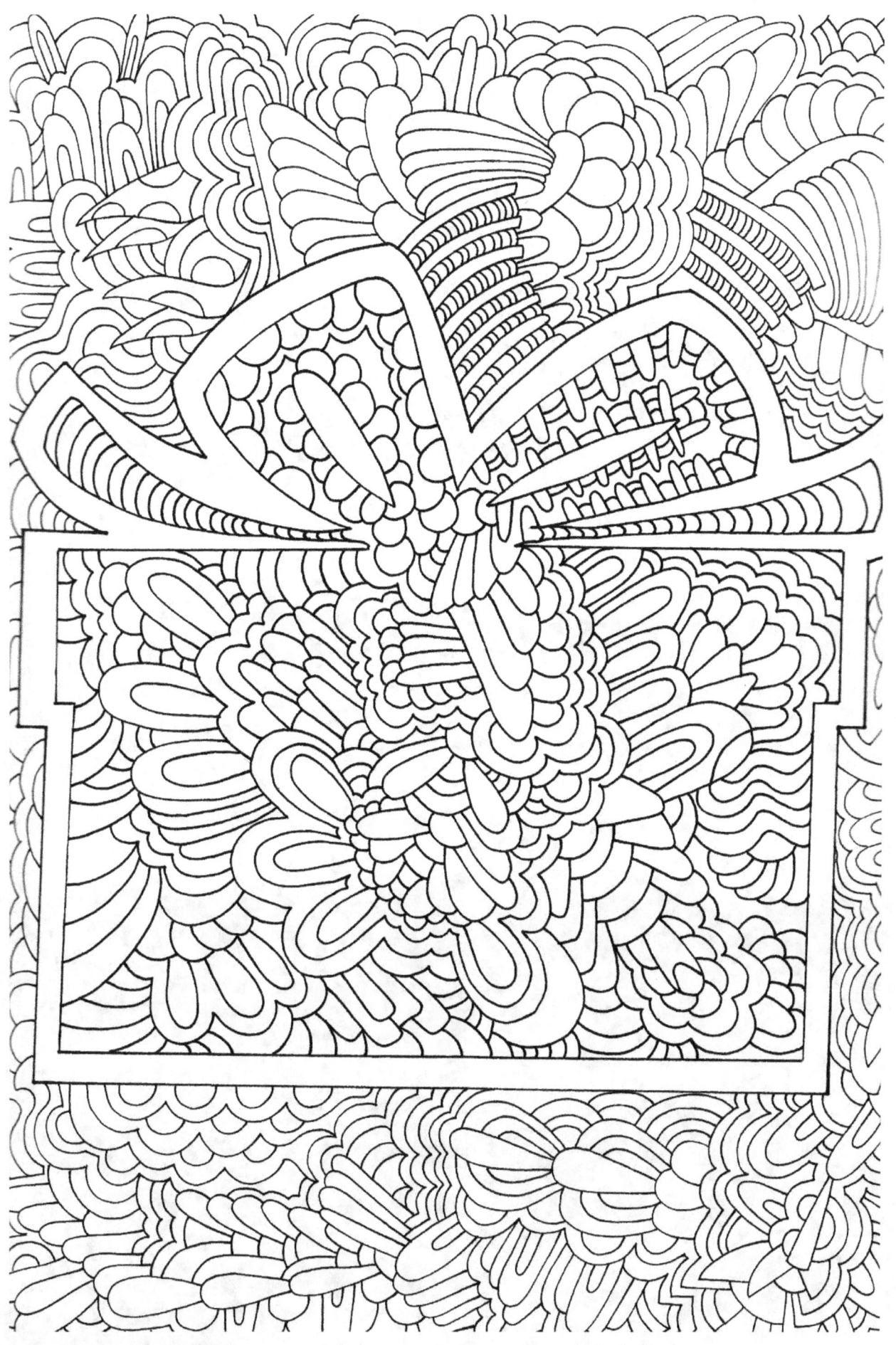

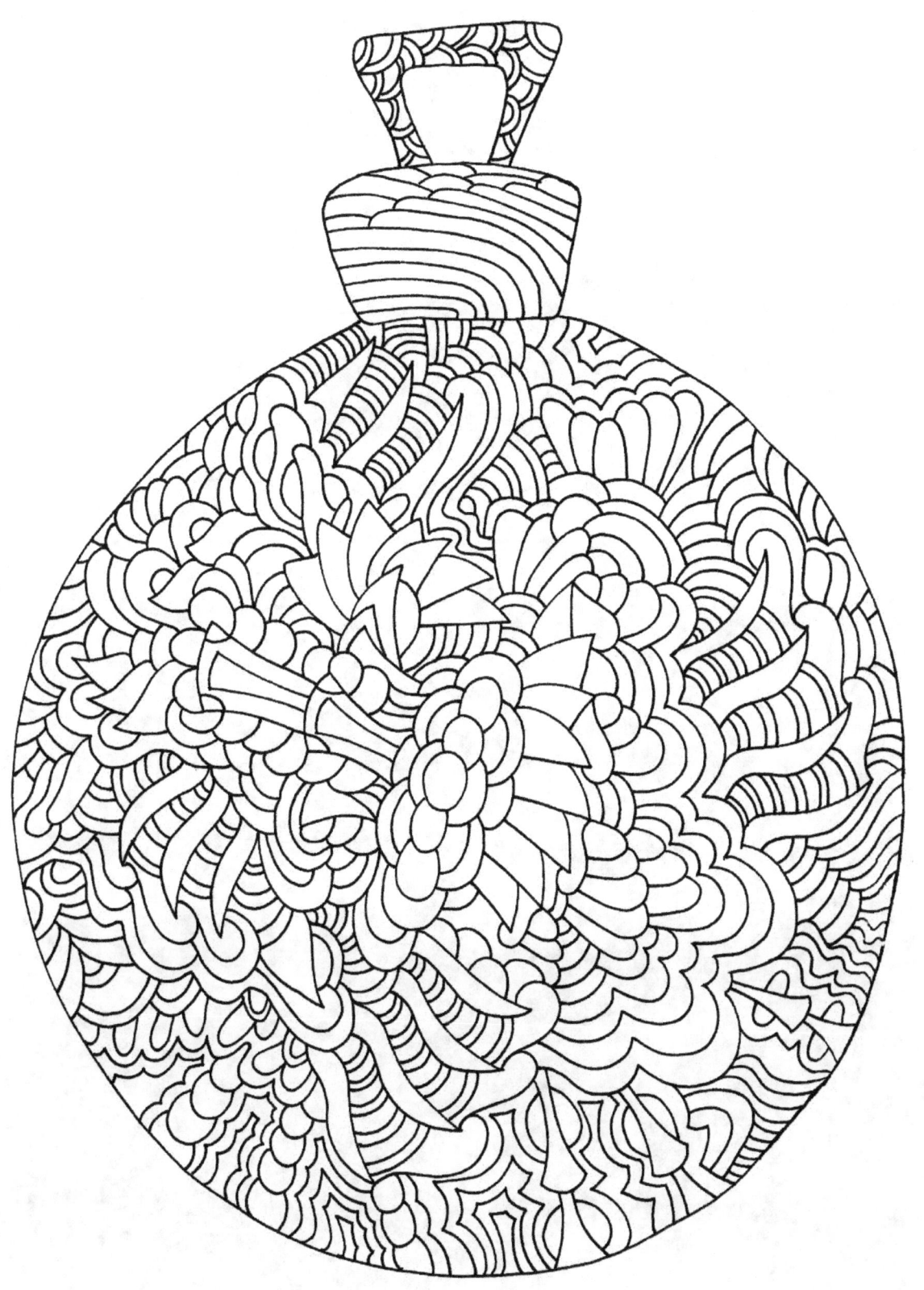

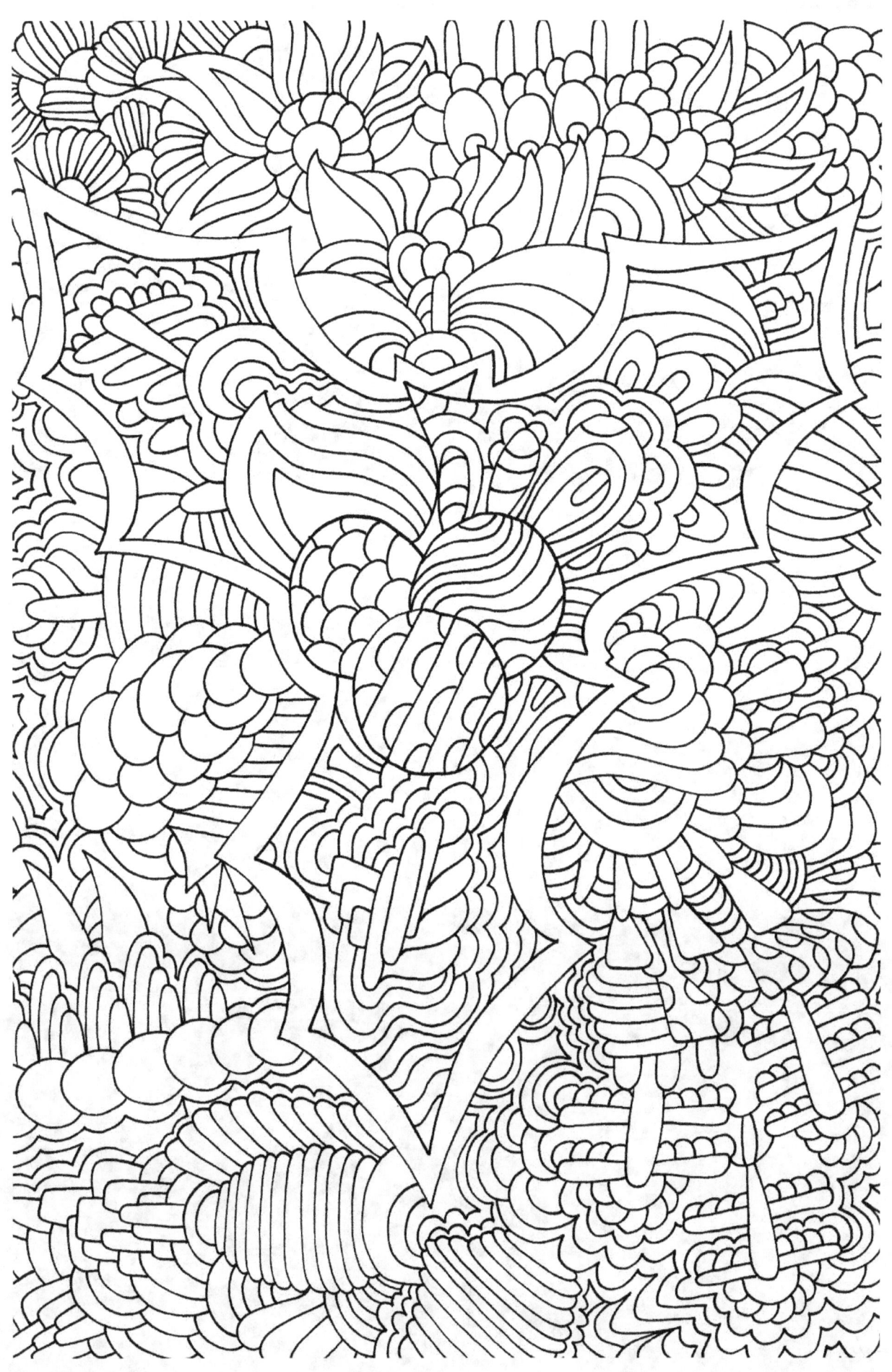

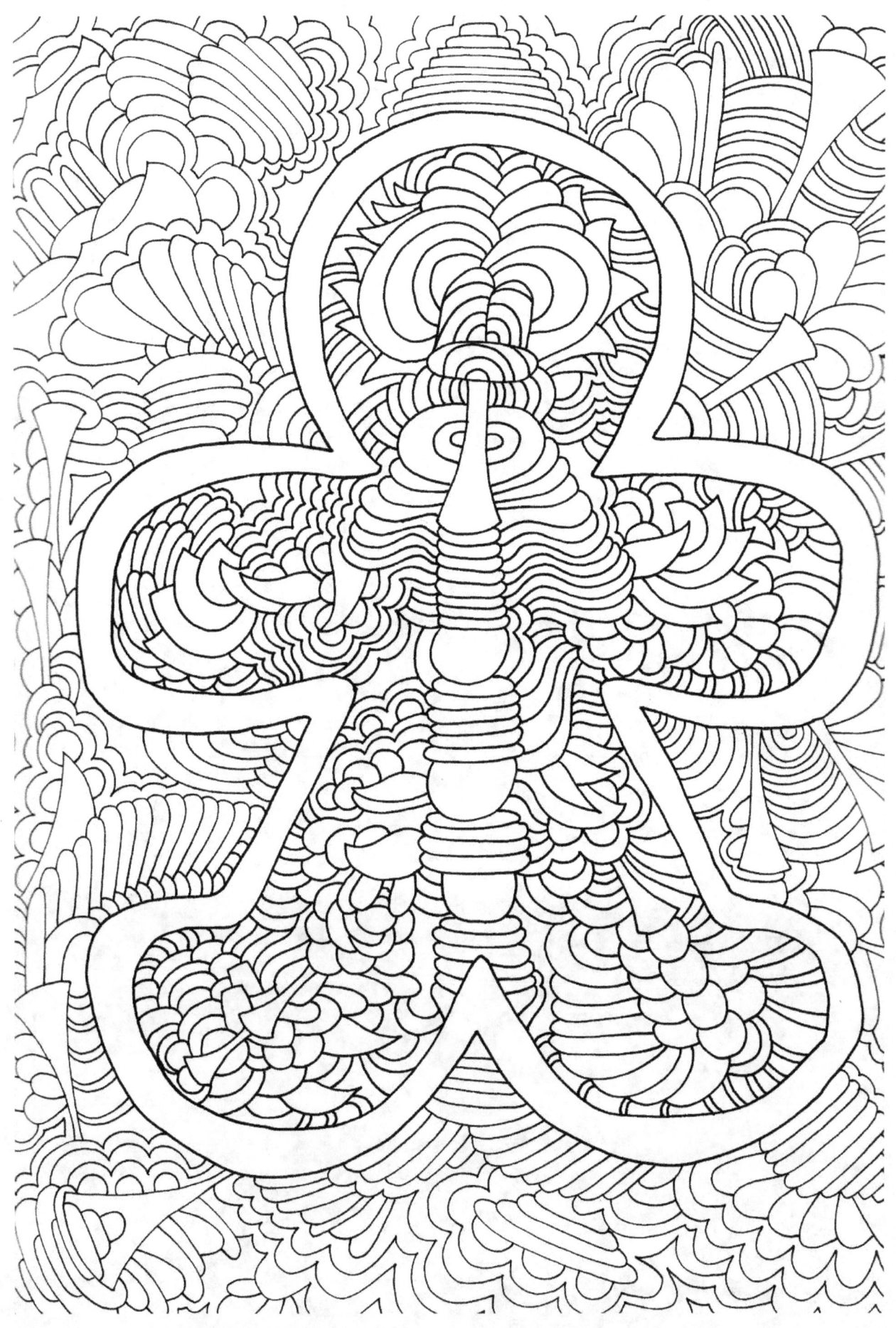

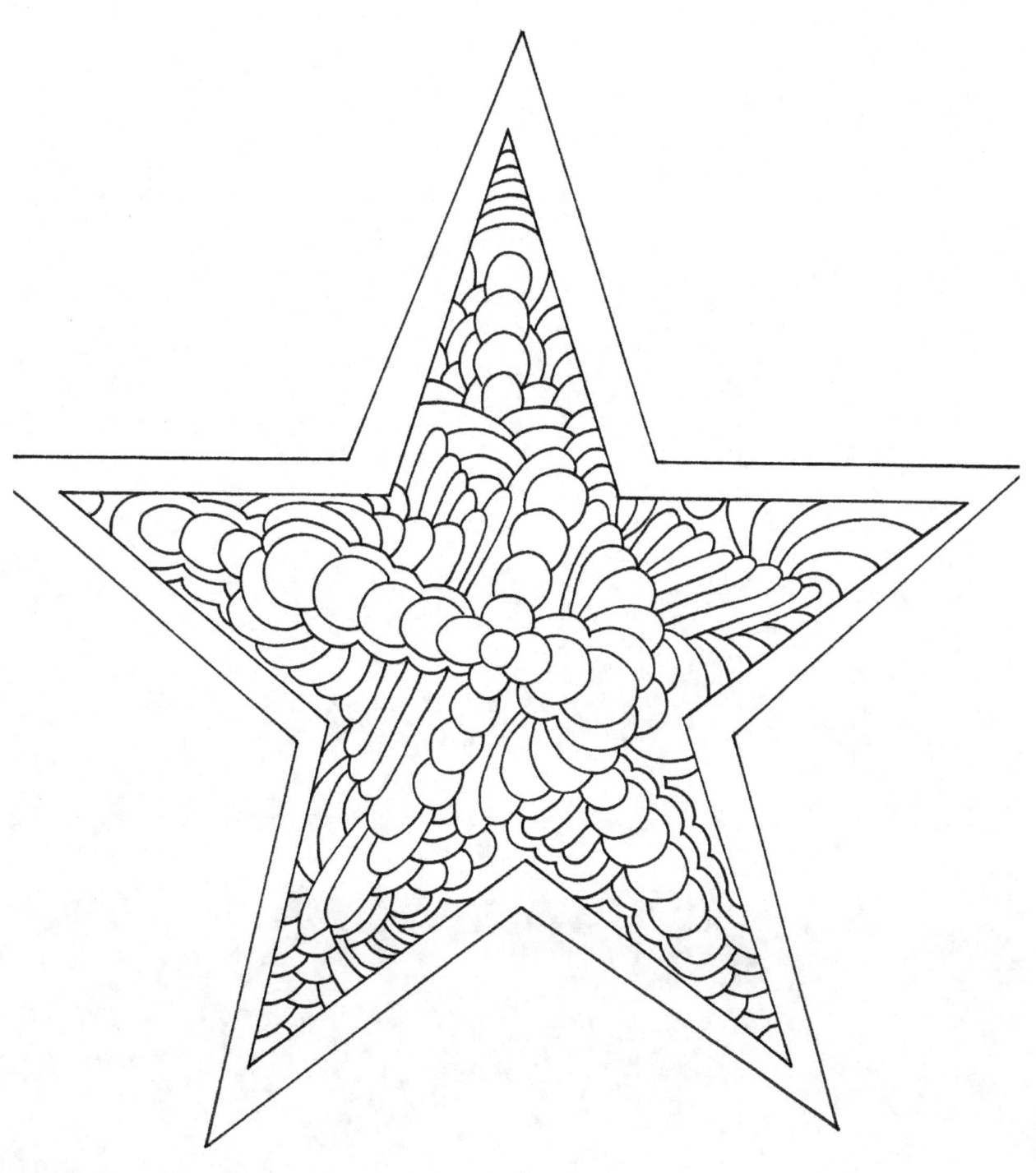

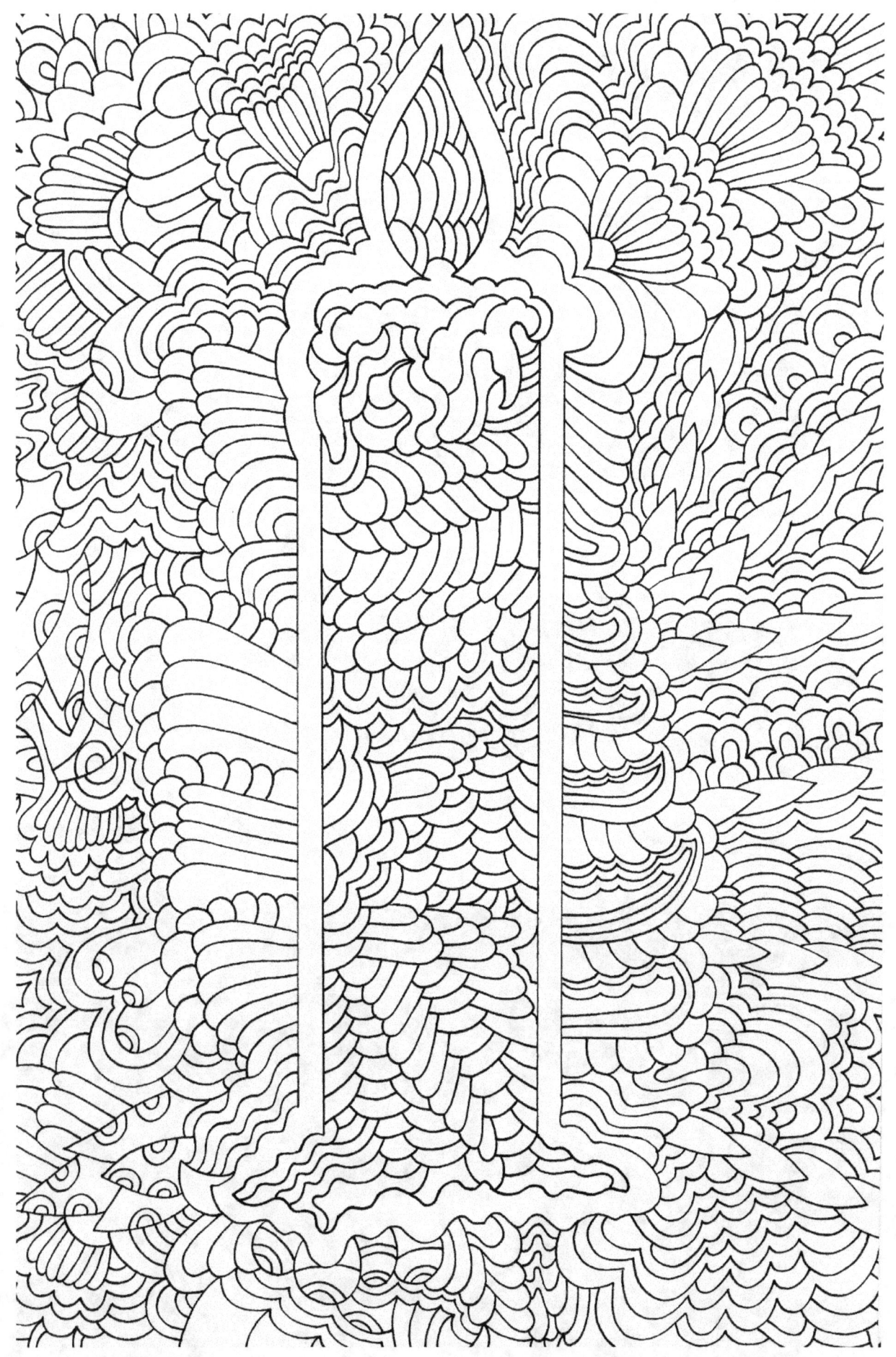

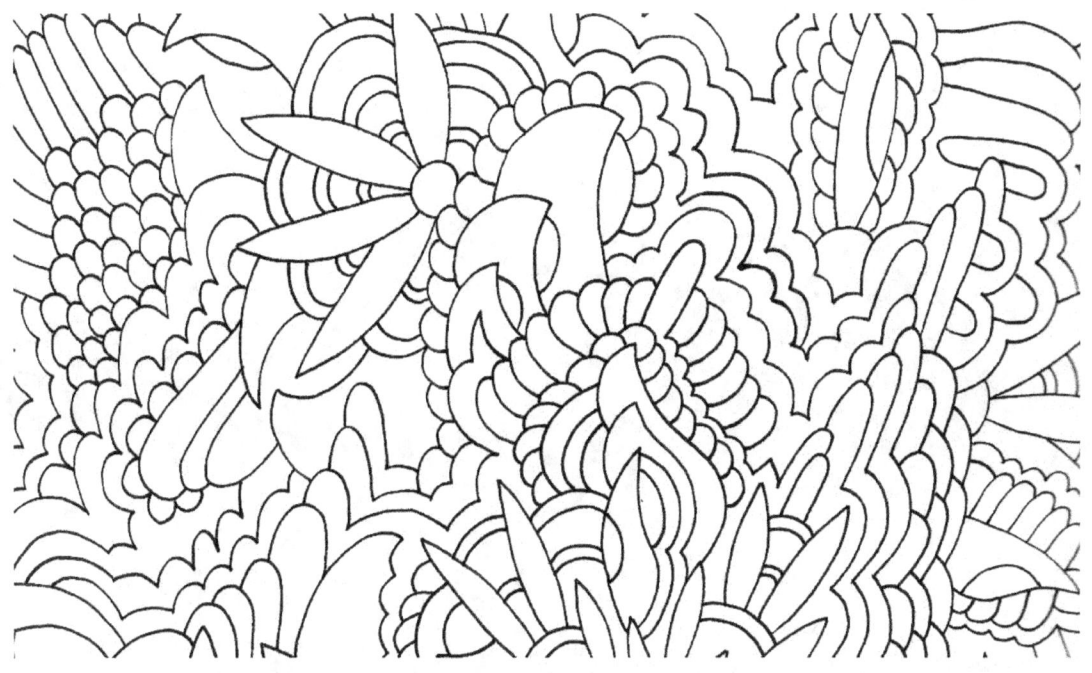

Hand drawn for you to colour at Christmas

aggiebrazil@gmail.com

©Karen Woodhouse 2016

www.ingramcontent.com/pod-product-compliance
Lightning Source LLC
Chambersburg PA
CBHW081304180526
45170CB00007B/2553